The Dying Gaul

By the same author

THE DARK EDGE OF EUROPE

DESMOND O'GRADY

The Dying Gaul

MacGibbon & Kee

First published 1968 by MacGibbon & Kee Ltd
3 Upper James Street Golden Square London W1
Copyright © Desmond O'Grady 1968
Printed in Great Britain by
Western Printing Services Ltd, Bristol

SBN: 261.62121.1

For Leonard-Jules and Deirdre O'Grady

There grows from the root of wrong the
flower of suffering.

AESCHYLUS : *The Choephori*

Man must suffer to be wise.

AESCHYLUS : *Agamemnon*

Report me and my cause aright.

HAMLET

The Dying Gaul

I

The day delivers her burden. The year
achieves renewal. In expectant towns
each ghosted hearth honours the one sky father.
The first heard bell is St. John's.

This ancient earth, these laboured lands,
announce love's annual mystery. The great
mother bears her own salvation—though man's
cross remains his seasons, his people, his death.

Rejoice in the chosen child's promise,
record his deeds as they're done.
Proclaim this day the marked man's praise
who cannot stay with us long.

2

The words, mythological waifs, wait
already written in memory—
only need reassembling, strength
from captive souls and to be
pronounced, as words over a ritual act . . .

Our cradle marks our grave
and cave.
Three-faced all in one
we must be born thrice.
Our birth stays subterranean
life in death—save
she, bearing, dies.

Delivered from death
We're licked by the fire of it.

Grown up gone
elsewhere, in the hour of our prime
what's divine becomes human,
the human divine.

We might sing it
given the tune.

3

The young sun, like the clear-toned swan,
swells to its appointed solstice. In spring fields
the engendered earth fattens root, stalk and flower.
He grows into his own coherent energy, inherits his burdens.

The early fosterage and training, the hour's ultimate approach
like a sacrament or taking arms, now achieves confirmation.
He stands a lone castaway in grief's unique nobility:
mortal, unknowing, terrified man.

His state established, his plighted action clear,
he performs the ritual of all ancient dance,
all ageless struggle, condemned to lose—for the world's
been bartered away, save from the ikon of his savaged face.

4

I

Summer has come. The splendid sun exults.
Down through the valley's deafness
the male river thrusts. Man in his strengths
and graces exalts his body's dust. His horses
crop the plain's fat clover.
His woman's a mother.

II

His city rises, a blaze out of the river's
sweep to the sea. Walls,
steeples and fortress burn sheet metal. The wider
streets, alive as bazaars, look a panic of prodigals
from the pure heat of their houses,
the times' abuses.

III

At the green mouth of the river the sea's
in flood. The wind sets
from the west and the spirit of the wanton wave flies the shore's
white banner. The tide's at the full and the wind conflicts
with the sand in the estuary. For miles
his seacrow caws.

5

Night burdens the bedroom's
body. The sleeping woman
dreams.
Out of her nightmare's
pregnant belly a viper
crawls.
With all the care of a mother
she wraps it up
in her shawls.

The snake in his hunger
suckles.
His fang draws blood
in clots.
The woman wakes in terror,
screams for protection,
lights.

Reality restores
uneasy reassurance.
The threat withdraws—
perhaps.

6

The season swells, the snails
climb out of ground.
When the crane flies south the fallow land
is broken. The farmer sows

while his earth's still light and scalds
his bins and cauldrons
of old cobwebs. Clay and corn is
packed in the earth like moulds.

The dead excess of growth
is cut and burnt.
He gives his child a name as ancient
as his people's earth.

He drinks the fruit and eats
the meat he lives on.
This is his speech and these his deeds,
this his ageless communion.

7

The wind sets from the west and the sun
declines from its solstice. The sailor shoves keel
to breaker, his broad sheet wide open,
and settles his course to the wave's tumble.

Far from the land, tabooed ages thick
by wind and wave, he consumes consecration
from the high heather sun and burns like a wick
in that isolation which confirms his protection.

All crossing water involves a search
and a maturation: a vision of the imagination,
relief from our daily griefs, a reach
for an answer, or its equipment, to act upon.

The foreign harbour made, the boat
fast prow and stern, the voyager's in another
world. When he returns he'll relate
what he's seen and learned, to help kill the winter.

8

This old man who inhabits the harbour's café table
drinks his blood-red wine from a glass between us. At his age
now, neither male nor female, and blind to the venal,

he delights in reading the world's mad signs with the gauge
of a wise man's inward view and interpretation.
He talks of the times and the cause of the times' misusage . . .

'As an age ebbs into decline, the release in motion,
the increase of freedom, threatens survival on the times'
tide. If a man cannot chart his true position

he's lost. Yet the answer's as fatal. He condemns
himself outright by learning too much, like Narcissus, and pays
with his life for that view of his image in alien streams.

Though we all must one day meet our killer demon,
chance all in combat, lose all and die,
our loss still burns in trophies, yields our freedom . . .'

The old man, done, draws back into his shadows,
says no more. The light dies with the sun.
The evening's figures float past before my eyes.

9

At the tip of my reaching finger,
out of their tumulous past, I evoke their image:
a mythology of shadows migrating
west from the Caucasus, and Anatolia, raiding
across the pastures of Europe for forage

and settlement—a darkly massed caravan of horse,
oxen and swineherd—with their shaft-hole axe
and the blockwheel. Again, from that complex
Greece and the Balkans, the progress

of copper and bronze to the Danube.
Later, with iron for weapons and farming,
they surveyed the Atlantic and settled, sleeping
easy at night, with the strength of the family group

built out of cattleherds, the spoils of war plunder
and a man's battle price for his honour.
In time came fine goldwork, an oral tradition,
a myth and a magic, and manuscript illumination.

Their image fades to an ember.

The reaching hand withdraws as the times digest
their tomb. Another image emerges. I become aware
of a grotesque family: my aged father, his child-worn woman
and my lone daughter weeping under dishevelled hair.

The wizened woman's of the western sea. Her crabbed face
bends to her knees and her body's all
dropped. She must take the rags of her garments
even into the sun, now her time is at hand for renewal.

Her grey-headed husband, his years cut down like trees
about him, has come into his age's humiliation.
Daily the thread of his brain unravels. He approaches
his last just rage, his final regeneration.

Out of the sacred heart of his ancient affection, his virgilian
voice puts the words into my head: the adoration
of that mystery which makes the life of the world; the chance
of this in the gifts given to man and man's endurance.
The whole image is over.

10

The day dawns and the morning star
shines like ice. The Festival of August
and the three phases of the gestate year
deliver their full maturity at last.

This land in its growth and increase gives
man his plenty and the storm safe sea
his shoals. Farmer or fisherman he rises
to celebrate abundance and I my birthday.

At thirty odd I confront my quarry,
my sacrifice—the need to keep this grievous
green world from dying—aware I alone carry
the perennial urn that contains my own ashes.

Long headed, back-swept hair
abundant, he's tall as timber,
hard as hobnails.

Loose-limbed, muscular
as marble, his spiked white
hair could impale falling apples.

You might say he has three faces
with a name for each—
brazen as bronze—
for the power of its sake.

His lip carves a curve
could carry glorious moustaches
with caucasian grace.

His arm's long, far-reaching.
His strength gathers to noon
declines at evening.

He stands sundered from his land.

Sent down to the godly sea
he's walked foreign harbours,
seen the other world, known
its women.

Back,
he's used what he's learned
to slaughter the winter, bring on
spring labour with the healer
touch.

He may pass at will
through paddocks of light—
and he harbours concern
for the loser.

Blood and spirit
bound, hold—
a knot.

He's a pentacle of a man.

I 2

A mad male-hearted woman in a prouder age
swore she'd see her husband under first,
she plotted so, and did. She scorned his marriage
bed from then and swept her dead man's dust
clean from her mind and memory. The trait's remained
a hidden threat since down through her tainted lineage
and the more it's hidden the more it's deep ingrained.

I walk the ruins of our old house and survey
my grim inheritance, my native right, and call
to its ghost for sanction. Old stones are tongues, they say,
of the unquiet dead and no man's house will fall
without due reason. What was done in my absence that I should find

my father's image struck shattered from the wall
and a scarecrow's brain replace his hawk-like mind?

All ruin bears witness, the stones cry out the price
of all uprising. The noble perish, lost
for the times' demands. The base still rule, increase
their lot upon advantage, cull the cost
and sell all gain back to the old deviser.
Not by strangers but by our own we're crossed
and murdered—in the name of the father, the son and the mother.

13

Always, when at odds
with this unmelting flesh, its fever's sweat,
when all my dreams grow nightmares,
the pattern recurs: I vertigo, upset
and pitch to the same dread centre
where I confront your image, mother,

as though after a long and travelled absence.
You wait in your child-forsaken rose garden—
gaudy in a long red gown as an evil goddess.
Beside you an ass and cart, your token
chariot.
All innocence seems deprived you. The scarlet

eyebrows of your looking face
arch as you grin grotesquely.
At his usual remove, in his appointed place
like your shadow, I also see
the shape of your companion—that crude cowherd
driving the butchered bull-calf onward.

My father is never present. Later, in the stale
damp sheets of waking, the fever less,
your dreaded presence passed, I fail
to manage reason. I nurse
incessant doubt all over—fear an inherited share
of you, like a flaw, will call my final number.

The daily drudge or drama is not of weakness
but of such generalities as duty,
self-denial, the culpable degree of guilt. I sense
I gradually grow unbalanced from exaggeration. Put my
crime down to omission—
doing nothing to prevent one man's declension.

In the deeper reaches of the race
and family, mother, a son naturally
harbours a mute ambition, as the books say, to replace
his house's head, his father—silently
condones whatever gets it done.
No man should fully trust his son.

14

The pitch piles up in part
on part of the heart's abyss.
Unbalanced from exaggeration
I career towards crisis.

Blood gangs up in the groin.
Nerves knot at the temples.
In one flush fury thrusts
and the wall of reason tumbles.

The eye rolls out of orbit.
The body bucks like a beast's.
Driven daft by his dream
the whole man bursts.

Spannered, the works
fly all over the shop:
wardrobes, women, babies,
bedrooms, kitchens—scrap.

In bits
things mean more
terribly themselves—
undone for.

I pick, prefer,
accept, adopt
just like a feather sorter
in his feather loft.

The blindness over,
bleakness stretches out
empty as an ocean
round one small boat.

But something's always had it,
burnt out, destroyed;
for whatever new comes from it
something old died.

15

Sacred heart,
house of gold;
visioned girl,
hag;
love or death;
in that land
I so resemble
seem two mouths
joined invisibly—
an animal's cave.
Hide against iron and stone,
she ravages yearly
her young.

Daily,
with my bare hand,
I throttle her life
and my own.

Far from the land,
barred from the town
I do what I'm told
at a distance—
condemned for life
to her skin and bone.

16

Like that beast
of classic times
today's monster's
as many-headed.

Temptation's
to join, even enjoy
him—head
by honourable head.
Most do.
The few
make a fight for it.

Plundering like power, he's a pusher—
angels, engines, you name it—
eats men like air
singly, in groups, whole nations.

Knock him?

Burning him off like a wart,
burying him under a rock
you stand some chance.

17

Quirky from inquietude,
on the loose again,
free as young blood
bulling for bacon,
I loped the land
killing for food or fun
like an animal.

Knew what I wanted—
no man better. Went after it
many a wild sea mile
well equipped with my golden
twig and tinkling bells.

Sighted, I stalked her a year,
tired and took her alive
whacked from her own involvement—gold-
templed, bronze-bucking.

Now she's night
noon and morning mine
and her protection.

18

A butty man,
uncle wore black;
had nailhead eyes,
hid in the house of himself.

For me, a child,
he loomed hugely homeric:
stories, history.
Yet I never heard him sing.

Father replacer
he outbulked mine.
Mastered my day
a long time.

Outgrown it
I still baulked,
couldn't shift—had
to inhume his image.

Shrunk now
he's silent,
and odd.

Father avenger
I'm freer.

19

When heaven stoops his fire
it's steerage away on the nightferry . . .

Ashore in the northern night
you're herded in tribes onto trains
for industrial cities and camps
as the Jews were for Auschwitz, Buchenwald, Belsen.

In worker ghettos
you scoop cesspools and sewers;
shovel shit, slop and slagheaps;
build towns, roads, general transport;
crawl home at night
a cockroach
charred black as the Negro
by the Man's furnace.

Crowds chuck in, levelled. Many
get knocked off quickly early on.
With luck you get out,
leave the lot behind
as in mass graves.

All said and done
you feel cleansed, strengthened;
shove out south toward sun,
survival—
unforgetting,
unforgiving.

20

Faithful, you've waited—
like an angel who's been
on the road beside me all the time. I
return shaken from the hard-hearted north.
Explaining it to you this lovemaking
night I gather your courage for tomorrow's
continuance, realise the simple
enormity of your protection.

Always you show
the strength of relentless
honesty over all opposition,
expense, suffering;
nor shall I ever doubt the firm
ease, vitality, of your devotion.

The fowl of various death
attack daily—
mute and molest without mercy.
Bent on succession, youth
urges age on to crisis, wives
renegue and the crone of indulgence
reduces the lot to her image.
Out of this, daily deliver me.

2 I

Powerful as prophecy,
ominous as a medieval Order
false jesus came from the sea
bellowing fire and death
as a bull plunder.

We met where my town
rises out of her river's
sweep to my ocean—
fields all flowers,
orchards.

As boys
we danced to his whim,
felt the graze of his horn.

I killed him one night
on my own
and cleared out of town—
unknowingly dragging his ghost along.

22

Serenity structures
the equiline bone,
her horsey head—
as the song built
into the instrument
playing it does.
                    Like cavalry,
she'll always carry the day.

More than I
have considered that part—
as an onlooker
outside the unchecked,
haywire hedge.

Each horse jaw
face may be skinned away
to the palour
of the peeled mushroom—
and the skeleton
still find its own prairie.

At times you may trot
the filly home.
But who minds the mare
or cleans and stocks the stable?

23

I

Condition ? Present
but second hand.
Spancelled.
At halt.

Some moves are imposed,
others free.

I I

In Nature's design
holes have importance.

As a boatman rows
through the gap
between land and sky,
I push out, remove, to a rock
of pause, indecision.

I I I

Something between the stupid
stone and dumb wave
contains, yet cods, binding,
protection.

Girt with dead
familiars—every corpse
cries out for a cock—
I return equipped
with what's wanted.

IV

But combinations shift,
alter at resistance—
skin like snakes,
change as clouds.
Everything's dragged in, used.

V

In the wind-up
one gets knocked off,
the other
turns necrophilic.

24

Set out,
I sailed steadily
into the sun—
sinking like a fiery
mythological dragon
wound round some sacred tree
or treasured loot—
and found
a sepulchral land.

My task: to free
my days of their dragon,
to sever his tree
at the root,
establish my own
alien alphabet,
return.
Done, my reward
was wife and family
bed and board.

25

The season ripe, wild
geese yearly form and fly
to some mysterious field
behind the north wind
and the sun's scalded eye.
Many a madman's followed
suit. One year so did I.

I found and faced
a hundred headed monster
looked like an oracular ghost.
Every head spoke a language
and on his long-suffering shoulder
he bore his burden of a cosmic cage

With crude apprentice patience
I served my time to his trade,
learned the hundred ways of his life's lunations.
When he's gone and I claim my legacy
from his three-faced serving maid
I'll be ready to travel freely
through paddocks of light and the dead.

26

Today's task
sheers tougher than yesterday's—
though they're all
black ballaksed anyway.
And every raw
start or conclusion is well
watched by its own
particular horror
like a wolfhound.

At worst
all's singlehanded,
starkness,
and no help allowed
from exterior forces—
catharsis!

At best
three seasons
maket it.
The rest,
for foreign reasons,
forget!

27

Like some undreamed-of phantom,
with my own pampered differences—but not
unlike her fool-child the mother
hoards buried out of sight
mowing in his own filth
until enclosure and that madness
kill and rid him—I daily
roam from room to spying room
beardy, mat-haired, listless and unwashed
as a beggar or robber-tramp
seen on the open road
or at the back door
of a big house.

Gulping air,
grinning foolishly at times,
I alternate planned silences
with rehearsed speeches, obscure jokes
and riddles. Alone or in company
I rattle them off deliberately—
against women mostly
and their marriages.
I hint unholy crimes, unholy punishments,
delight in foul, abusive language
and provoke heartscald tears,
cowed confessions, distracted pleas,
suicidal forces.

Slovenly at meals, I slop and slobber
like a hog, fart and burp
at gleeful random. Too witless
to sound dangerous I guffaw
to see my brother hanged,
my father put to death at home,
and suffer in silent pretence
not to see—
enduring.

Stalked by the past for witness,
filing back like gravestones,
crazed by brute images, pale shadows
at their odds in this demented head,
I grope like a vertigo in terror
pushed daily out to that dark edge
of the heart's land's end
with its vision of ceaseless agony
far below for an answer.

Doubt hovers like a hawk
above the mind's abyss.
Trapped hesitant, Nature
stiffens in paralysis.

Baffled, I pause, caught
between what's definite
what disguise.

Who am I?

28

The living cry to the dead
wasting breath.
The dead, alive in their graves,
kill the living in their turn.

Back unexpected
after my itinerant
absence, you show terror
at my change; look at me
as one might a released
prisoner returned with a purpose
like revenge, or a beggar
recognized at the door
for a long lost child or love—
in either case
originally wronged.

Absence reveals, through the death
involved, the truth, the lie,
in what was left behind—
works the change.

Home, I'm alive and unforgetting.
Face to face for the pay-off
you fear unholy punishment.
My young word shall not prove false
and your one dignity, one house,
one love—your own—
shall get is one due death—
although they wrap a wreath of prayers
about my head.

False to the death,
you'll not live false to the Dead.
I end you in your pride.

29

The day concludes burning.
The north breathes like a dragon.

Held upright by a tree-stump
he fights what cannot die
but must replace him:
sun, sea, river,
moon and marketplace.

What's forceful beyond man
mounts up in one black-crested wave
and sweeps the sod between them.

Disevaluation of all value
bartered reputation,
disdained endeavour
flood forward for the kill
upon him.

Bulls of land and sea
lock in final combat.
Black confronts white.

Over his hanging head
his seacrow circles thrice
and settling on his shoulder
folds her wings,
caws.

3○

The hour at last come round
    the stroke that scores the kill
taken, there follows a painless,
        partly nostalgic withdrawal—
a drag to the sideline—to a clean piece
        of this world's dying ground.

Lean legs nerve like an athlete's.
        Raised kneecaps gleam altar marble.
Thigh shanks knot. The curled
        weighty balls bag low and the gentle
penis limps childless. Tousled,
        his head's like a young brown bull's.

Reclining, at repose upon
        one unwound nude haunch,
pelvis and dragged out legs
        draining, his belly's bunch
about the navel wrinkles.
        Life strains on his taut right arm.

The blood clots, the nerve
        sings and all his joints
jamb stuck. His grounded gaze,
        like the madman's private smile, confronts
the process' revelation—the ways
        death consummates, like love.

47

3 1

The black boar tusks his rage
through the levelled land. The black
seacrow at last claims the shore.
The year, at flood,
returns to its watery origins.

Wave,
beginning and end,
returns to primary wave.

The stake stands stuck
through the heart of the Dog.
Black overcrows white.
Pride beats out its brains on its quarry.

The marked child's promise, the wounded
name, acquitted, election
lights on the bull-calf seen in dreams
and cup and cauldron rise in consecration.

This harsh world draws one last breath
in pain
and stops—dead.

Severed head's held swapped for severed head.

Things standing thus
shall live behind
and memory live green
among some people.

32

Thought harder, heart keener,
mood more, as might lessens.

The match made has been met.
If much fell in the effort,
much scattered and given away
to the world, our thoughts still remain
in the encounter.

Though speech be spectral
word becomes deed,
deed word.

The trouble of love
is no loss of labour
and it's blindness for anyone
arranging a confrontation
to set aside the confrontation with Death.

Desirous of renown,
our consolation is the praise and esteem
of a few fellows—
through what merits their honour
do we prosper . . .

The rime-crusted boats that bear
the what's left of us leaving,
are sailing.
On the western wave
the sun sets.

Heaven swallows our smoke.

Such a sight becomes the field.

33

Death dazzles death.
Fertile, the fire of it
shall grave a living monument . . .

Winter's grip weakened,
the northern lights withdraw;
the dead land's spirit
stirs in thaw.

All shadows merge on the centre,
limbs clasp in a ring;
the makers of longing enter,
dance again.

The dead unburdened, the year's
renewed. Man,
avenged, declares:
I am my father's son.